ACKNOWLED(

Thanks are due to the publi
these poems first appeared: *The ~~Open Ear, Channel, Empty~~
House* (Doire Press, 2021), *Bee Safe Bee Zine, Firewords,
The Tangerine, Poetry Ireland Review, Unpredictapple, No
Offence, Monstrous Regiment, Hello I Am Alive* (Poetry
Ireland, 2019), *The Blackbird* and *Queering the Green:
Post-2000 Queer Irish Poetry* (The Lifeboat Press, 2021).

Thanks also to the Seamus Heaney Centre, to my MA
classmates and to my tutors (past and present) whose
careful feedback made the poems in this pamphlet
possible – Andy Eaton, Sinéad Morrissey, Leontia
Flynn, Paul Maddern and Gail McConnell. Thank you
to Stephen Kelly, who taught me nothing about poetry
but much besides.

Thank you to my editor, Emma, and to my therapist,
Emma (no relation), both of whom have worked hard
to massage my thoughts into something usable. Thank
you to the unstoppable Toby Advocates – Fionn, Orla,
Kieran, Izzy, Jeni, Rob, Jan, Rosamund, Lena, Mícheál
and many more. Thank you to my family, friends and
antagonists. Thank you to Conor for still being here.

Thank you to those I didn't get around to thanking
properly – Ciaran, Eavan and Granfer.

MILKsNAKE

POEMS BY TOBY BUCKLEY

THE EMMA PRESS

THE EMMA PRESS

First published in the UK in 2022 by The Emma Press Ltd.
Poems © Toby Buckley 2022.

ISBN 978-1-912915-98-9

A CIP catalogue record of this book
is available from the British Library.

Cover design by Amy Louise Evans.

Printed and bound in the UK
by the Holodeck, Birmingham.

The Emma Press
theemmapress.com
hello@theemmapress.com
Birmingham, UK

CONTENTS

Our News

I don't remember blood
but sometimes screaming,
the feeling of being seven years old
and watching a boy put his hand
in a pencil sharpener.
The moment crystallises
into your retinas, at unexpected moments
shivering back into view.

Wallpaper-covered textbooks.
Jacks in the plasticine pot.
A poster-paint crust hardening on a jar.
Miss Wheeler's coffee mug.
The boy's skin a discarded Elastoplast
on the desk beside us.

Inver

In the bay there were five or six
great dark floating monsters –
fish farms tended by men in RIBs
who threw down illegal lobster pots
and slung us Tesco bags of crab claws
not to tout. Our teas-with-powdered-milk
and Cup-a-Soup cup dinners
all tasted like boat, like purple
methylated spirits too pretty
to drink, and the dolphins all had gaps
and chunks missing and looked wrong and wild
and not like the real dolphins I saw
on TV. And their wet backs brushed
slimey against our feet and in school
I lied and made them magic,
kept the truth in the boot with the lifejackets.

Bufo

Scooped as an infant from the pond
in a Baresa tomato and bacon
pasta bake sauce jar, the young bellwether
enters its natural habitat: an old baby bath
in the back garden of a bungalow.
It's a lesson in the circle of life for families
who won't give in to the child's cry
for puppies, siblings or goldfish,
the young instead left to observe
with an analyst's eye as jelly becomes
tadpole becomes froglet, gurgling up
until the house comes under siege
by fifty or seventy-five tiny frogs
looking impossibly human, impossibly
like smears of dark toothpaste.
The smears glint and pulsate for days
on the lawn, in the flower pots.
Most are picked off by local cats;
the rest grow hastily into bumpy yokes
blinking their triple lids, blaring
their fleshy vocal sacs
and slipping into the family
wellies, left unguarded on the doorstep.
Weekly, their rubber diving suits

split across the belly and down
the back like artist smocks, shucked
and slurped into the wearer's mouth.
Their bodies are lungs, their ears
are timpani drums. Their loose skins
glitter. Their nuptial pads grow sticky.
The pasta jars are waiting on the shelf.

Waders

That summer one of the boys from the boats
tumbled overboard and paddled and sank,
washing up on St. John's Point days later
with his green boots still burping seawater.
They said it was the waders that did it:
the watertight rubber from toe to chest
gulps the sea, keeps it in and pulls you down,
an anchor strapped on with hi-vis braces.

And the boys from the boats kept their boots on,
knowing well the disrespect of learning
too quickly from another man's mistakes.
And the mackerel that summer kept biting,
and the nets were raised and lowered, all eyes
averted from the place the boy went in.

Men Gathering Honey

Araña Cave, Valencia

The men are naked from the neck
down, protected in no way

from bee-stings, grass-cuts
or ropeburns. They

straddle a rudimentary
ladder of esparto grass

(which is plentiful in this region)
and reach for a hole in the rock face.

Archaeologists think the sack
of honey they carry is made

from some sort of skin.
Around the men on the rock

gigantic bees tumble out,
all heads and bellies and wings.

They are worried for their queen.
The men are worried for their honey,

lower it gingerly down
their ladder for magic, religion,

alcohol or just something sweeter
than flesh to eat. We don't know exactly

when men began to eat and drink
bees' honey, but it was more than ten

thousand years ago and long
before farmers were invented.

Cold Today

I don't know if the air is hitting the birds
the same as me, that type of cold
where all the muscles in your back and between
your guts feel like they'll never get loose again,
like *this is my life now*. I imagine
it must make flying a challenge. In the morning,
the sun seems to forget to give us the time of day,
but in the afternoon, the clear sky
hints at a moon like the residue
from a round sticker you couldn't peel
off quite right.

Nostos

A battered tent and camping chairs
lie deserted in a field
near the West Somerset Railway line,
their owners' camping trip cut short
by a mysterious something.
Local horses have ceased to hear
the clatter of the old steam train.
Chomp sootladen grass. Nicker. Snort.

I find myself most nostalgic
surrounded by stuff from before
my time, fetishize the pastness
of it all. In compartments, our tea
arrives in style, speckled thick
with soot. I expect nothing less.

Companion

Bleary
from sleep and warm
water and no glasses
I spot an uncertain comma
sliding

he drags
his tail up my
shower wall cumbersome
and not unmaggotesque and I
can see

his guts
or maybe it's
his dinner I lean in
and squint for a better view of
his face

the boy
is spotty and
bean-legged like a young
caterpillar but uglier
I don't

know how
he got in here

I can't feed him this boy
will just have to fend for himself
naked

and damp
I slither out
a pupa but with lots
more limbs and leave my companion
to wash.

Entryway

I have had bad experiences
of things
going inside of things –

sometimes words
slipping into my open ears,
or boy things going inside
like wrong jigsaw pieces
leaving the smaller piece
sad and dogeared.

One time a moth
crawled into my
ear in the middle
of the night.

I had to spend six
hours in A&E
and when the doctor tried
to pull it out, he cut open my
ear canal

and I couldn't go in
the sea for two
to three weeks.

Pip

Despite the absence
of light or air, there's
a seed in my gut
and it is growing
to a sapling. Sharp,
budded branches rise
like Here, teacher! hands
prodding dainty blackheads
through my semolina
skin skin. Deep in
my surfaces, leaves
somehow transpire,
push against my flesh
to make it new and alien.
The stomata on my scalp
and other secret places
cough and pucker out
fat droplets of grease,
and I squeak the first
bulge of a chubby pink
apple in my neck.

Arils

A number of curious discrepancies about the pomegranates in lore and medicine make the story of Persephone's kidnapping incomplete. First, according to legend, Persephone ate the pomegranate; the medical writings indicate that pomegranate was administered as a suppository. - John M. Riddle, *Eve's Herbs: A History of Contraception and Abortion in the West*

Only when it is plucked,

portioned and toothpicked out

individually

is a pomegranate

appreciated right.

Its jacket – orange-red,

leathery, an onion

abashed at a punk bar –

lifts to secret geodes

of pulp-swaddled seeds. Fingers

fumble to regather

every translucent

red cornalike for forks

and cocktail sticks. To leave

these gems in their dull sack

is inconceivable,
is to ban a growing
girl from her five-a-day.
We can only assume
that Persephone's sin
was to enter the fruit
the wrong way.

Meliteus

One of Zeus's better names
was Melissaois: 'Bee-Man'.
He had a son by mistake
with a nymph who hid the infant
in the woods and got bees
to keep him sweet.
They kept him safe
and let him feed and by the time
the shepherd Phagros stumbled
on the child, he was amazed
at his rotundity.
Unsure of his parentage,
the shepherd called
his honeypot son 'Meliteus',
after his sugary guardians.
Soon young Mel was a hero
– like many young Greeks –
having completed any number
of daring deeds never written down.
He formed a town and named it
Melita, the honey-town,
for the bees who let him eat.

Shaping Staff

The first thing I learned at university
was that boiled sausages are almost healthy –
an alternative to their fried selves.
They taste similar, but now their skins slick off:

sad and prophylactic. I would like to see
what forces could do the same weird thing to me:
make me guiltless and lean, and let me shed my skin.

If I picked a shape I think I'd like to be
a snake, a milk snake, or really any form
of lovable snake. I'd leave ghosts of myself
everywhere. I'd leave them like you leave footprints.

Getting to Know You

Online, I read the local museum's collection
of insects was the second largest
in Ireland, and that it held over
a quarter of a million specimens.

I went to try and find them,
but counted only a hundred or so,
mostly moths and bees.
It bugs me, living

near so many creatures I haven't met.
I worry that if I went to my neighbours
for a cup of sugar, they might open the door
and all tumble out at once.

It'd be so embarrassing.
I am so sorry, I'd say. *I didn't mean to interrupt*,
and I'd gesture vaguely,
This.

Fog in the Emerald Necklace, Boston

after Fujiko Nakaya

Droplets have allegiances
to so much
we can't see.
Each cloud

builds itself
to curl and roll,
all particles,
all kissing and merging.

It's tough for us
to grasp our size,
the damage we do
to the round world.

And then the wind shifts,
and the sculptures are blown
to the north
as a waterfall.

Visits

The nurses told us she'd slept right through
the seat of her pyjamas – we brought more
but she thought the clothes hanger was a new
knife and fork, for when she had visitors

Her last words were a panicked whisper:
the foreign nurses were stealing her
sheep – canned tangerines – her slippers –
some of her socks – her possessions leaking

into some old lady market in the back of beyond
She had grown obsessed with the Asians
assigned to attend her, and with her son –
she said she didn't want his visits anyway

He'd been smuggling in more illegitimate
babies than she had room – or time – for,
she didn't have enough tinned fruit for all
the tiny dolls – please don't let him bring more.

Old Bones

My grandfather
horns
on his shoes
with a tablespoon
he cannot reach
his shoelaces
in the cold
kitchen the turkey
carcass is more
literal than chicken
the bigger bones
correspond
more readily
with a real animal
I think
I should really
be a vegetarian
and peel another
strip of the dark
meat from the base
of the bird.

Tree Forms as a Mother and Child

after Henry Moore

She's taller than physics
allows, ten times the height water
should climb before beginning to boil.
This doesn't bother her. If her pores were larger
she wouldn't be able to bring that water to her very top.
If she allowed a single bubble of air inside, all of her immaculate
tubing would be killed. She's the poster girl for intelligent design
Her freshest parts raise clear and high above the ground:
birds' nests, beehives, cocoons, baby squirrels, frisbees, secret huts
She is stronger than any one of us. The children often forget her
thick skin doesn't mean she isn't alive and vibrant, doesn't mean
she doesn't feel every word carved into the surface of her.
She brings us shade, shelter and fresh air
then lets us whittle her into something
more useful –
a chair
a table
a card
a model
of a tree
a beebox
a birdfeeder.

Oh, It's You

Today I found you secreted
in dusty Kodak clarity,
tucked into a cardboard packet
behind the china-kept-for-best.

You are grey and posing
with grey pets on a grey lawn.
You boast a bowl
of primroses on the doorstep.

You stroke a canvas, painting.
Here you have travelled
somewhere by helicopter ride
and the excitement is still

crinkling
your eyes.

Mischief

Where the rat goes
he sends us screaming
for our birdmasks. We have not
forgiven him for tropical
rat fleas and black death.

His body is an unrealistic
design of velveteen sack
over collapsible frame,
a breathing gazebo balancing
on the riverbank.

Each domesticated generation
shrinks his heart and brain.

The Curator

This spoiled room holds nothing but priceless coins,
coins on every countertop. Though a room adjoins
which employs crinoids – stony spirals – and bones
arranged neatly into their proper joints.
To this congress of odds and ends I am summoned,
made worthy with information, instructed to curate.
I take this task happily, the glamorous artifacts
matching no other miscellany around.

These are my only needs: specimens, curiosities.
A plaster cast hand, a wax dummy courtier,
a mummified queen: a gleeful morbidity
humming among eggshells and seashells
and scores upon scores of the finest dried
insects I have ever seen.

Pickling

My head under water in the bath sounds
the same as it does in every house
I've lived in, like heartbeats, muffled voices,
machines whirring far away.

In here, I must try hard not to think
about body parts jarred in formaldehyde,
but bends in the water make my vessel
look corpse-ish, bloated and wrong.

I am almost as hollow as a water wing
because when I breathe in my body
floats up to the surface but my base
stays on the bottom like a set of eggs.

It's a welcome sign that the sulphurous gases
haven't filled me, that I'm not yet rotten.

Sands

That rain can play games
of snake on the windows
of cars and trains
says an awful lot
about the air,
the metal carriage
constantly displacing
and replacing it in clumps
like a vast, tubular man
sliding into his morning
bath. The substance nudges
impatiently until
at last there is room
in the space left behind
the gone-train, fitting here
like it was never meant
to be anywhere
else. We see none of this
until a car ad pops up
and shows clean grains of sand
sweeping along a yoke
in an air tunnel.
It makes me wonder
how I would fare in such

circumstances, which
unnoticed dips
and dints would gather
the inappropriate sand,
which body part is best
to thrust forward first
on my journey through
the tube. I wonder
what impact this has
on my life without
me even noticing.

Portstewart, 25 March 2018

To think that – maybe in ten or twenty years –
we, too, could afford this: a flat
with a big window onto the sea,
a stone hawk whose feathers
are green and slick with algae,
a Marks & Spencers creme brûlée,
a glass bowl with keys and coins,
buttons from my shirt, pebbles you've found,
a dish of easy peelers, a bookshelf
with china turtles, penguins and seagulls,
a brown leather recliner three-piece suite.

ABOUT THE POET

Toby Buckley is an archivist and writer from Donegal, currently based in Belfast. He completed his MA in Creative Writing (Poetry) at the Seamus Heaney Centre at Queen's University Belfast as the first recipient of the Ruth West Poetry Award Scholarship. His work has appeared in numerous literary publications including *Poetry Ireland Review, The Stinging Fly, Channel Magazine* and the Doire Press anthology *Empty House* (2021).

ABOUT THE EMMA PRESS

The Emma Press is an independent publishing house based in the Jewellery Quarter, Birmingham, UK. It was founded in 2012 by Emma Dai'an Wright, and specialises in poetry, short fiction and children's books.

The Emma Press has been shortlisted for the Michael Marks Award for Poetry Pamphlet Publishers in 2014, 2015, 2016, 2018, and 2020, winning in 2016.

In 2020 The Emma Press received funding from Arts Council England's Elevate programme, developed to enhance the diversity of the arts and cultural sector by strengthening the resilience of diverse-led organisations.

Website: theemmapress.com
Facebook, Twitter and Instagram:
@TheEmmaPress